UNSOLVED
MYSTERIES
the secret files

Atlantis

Ann Lewis

the rosen publishing group's
rosen central

For my husband Joe, an enthusiast of all things mysterious

Published in 2002 by The Rosen Publishing Group, Inc.
29 East 21st Street, New York, NY 10010

First Edition

Library of Congress Cataloging-in-Publication Data

Lewis, Ann Margaret.
Atlantis / Ann Margaret Lewis.— 1st ed.
p. cm. — (Unsolved mysteries)
Includes bibliographical references and index.
Summary: Presents an overview of the mysteries surrounding the fabled civilization and island of Atlantis, including Plato's story, strange theories, and archaeological fact.
ISBN 0-8239-3559-0 (lib. bdg.)
1. Atlantis. [1. Atlantis.] I. Title. II. Unsolved mysteries (Rosen Publishing Group)
GN751 .L48 2002
001.94—dc21

2001004190

Manufactured in the United States of America

Contents

Many artists have drawn pictures of Atlantis based on folklore and legend.

1

The Legend Begins

Atlantis: The very name is fascinating, conjuring up images of fantastic wonders and horrible disaster. The story of Atlantis is even more intriguing. It tells of an extraordinary country of great wealth and achievement in learning, engineering, science, and war. This land, the story continues, sank into the sea in a great cataclysm of fire and earthquakes somewhere in the area of the Atlantic Ocean.

People have enjoyed stories about Atlantis for centuries. The island of an ancient golden age has spawned movies, television shows, novels, and comic books. But where does the original story of Atlantis begin? And is it based on truth?

Actually, we can answer part of the first question by looking at one man—the ancient Greek philosopher, Plato—who lived in the years 428 to 348 BC.

Plato was a student of Socrates, another great philosopher, who was forced to take his own life when his teachings about forming an

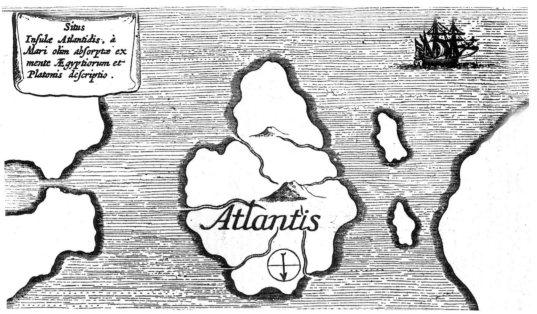

Early maps placed Atlantis in the middle of the Atlantic Ocean.

idyllic society started trouble with his government. Plato was sorely affected by his teacher's death, and was very much influenced by his thinking. And so Plato continued Socrates's teachings, writing extensively on the ability of man to create a society that is good for all people. One of his works, *The Republic*, details the nature of justice and truth, the role of art in education, and how government should serve the people. He revealed his views through a series of fictional conversations—called dialogues—between himself and several other philosophers, including his teacher Socrates.

The philosopher Plato is honored in busts. His account of Atlantis is the first in written history.

Plato created dialogues in all of his works, probably because he thought his teachings would be more easily absorbed by the reader this way. He first introduced the story of Atlantis in his dialogues *Timaeus* and *Critias.*

In *Timaeus*, Plato's friend Critias explains that a scholar named Solon (a real man who lived from 630–560 BC) passed the story down to a man named Dropides, who in turn told the story to Critias's grandfather (also named Critias). Critias says his grandfather told him the story, and that he came to recall it entirely after thinking about it overnight.

According to Critias, some Egyptian priests in a town called Saïs in the Egyptian Delta, told Solon the story of an island nation that had once lain in the Atlantic Ocean, just beyond "the Pillars of Hercules." The Pillars of Hercules are the Strait of Gibraltar, a treacherous sea passage connecting the Mediterranean Sea and the Atlantic Ocean, beyond which the Greeks did not sail. Critias reports that this mysterious lost nation arrogantly tried to attack the cities in Europe and Asia, and was held back. After that, violent earthquakes and floods destroyed it, and within a single day it sank beneath the sea.

Plato's *Critias,* written later, says something different from what was stated in *Timaeus.* Instead of claiming to have heard the story of Atlantis from his grandfather, Critias states that his father had a manuscript on Atlantis, which he studied often as a child. This is only one of the many inconsistencies to surface in the tale. Also, the fact that the story was passed down by a friend of a friend of a friend has caused scholars to scoff at the Atlantis legend for centuries.

Another fault scholars find with Plato's story is the date he says the destruction of Atlantis happened. According to Plato, the great tragedy occurred 9,000 years before he wrote the *Timaeus* dialogue. The people of Atlantis were said to have great gardens, splendid architecture, and amazing feats of engineering, from tunnels and bridges to racetracks and hot and cold springs. Yet the date that Plato gives for Atlantis would be far in advance of even the great civilizations of Egypt, the Near East, and India. In fact, according to known history, no civilization as advanced as the one that Plato describes existed so many thousands of years ago.

According to Plato, the construction of grand, elaborate tunnels was one of the hallmarks of Atlantis's advanced civilization.

Another theory that some researchers have introduced is that the place Plato called Atlantis influenced the birth of other great cultures, such as those of the ancient Egyptians and the Maya of Central America. The mysterious place Plato called Atlantis died, but survivors carried their culture to other places to start anew. This, they claim, would explain the mysterious way that cultures as far apart in geography and time as the Maya and the Egyptians developed similar forms of architecture and science, and how their cultures flourished in similar ways for thousands of years.

Is it possible that such a great civilization existed so long ago that it influenced the great peoples and the civilizations of Egypt, Greece, and the Western world that followed? To answer this question, we have to look in more detail at when Atlantis is said to have existed.

2
A Problem of Time

In his writing, Plato sets the destruction of Atlantis 9,000 years before his telling of the story, which would be approximately 9,500 BC. As we said in the previous chapter, this is a problem to most archaeologists and scholars, because as far as we know, there were no civilizations at this time of the type that Plato described. To illustrate how far back in time Plato was talking about, this is 3,000 years before the very first pharaoh of Egypt!

Maybe, as some scholars believe, Plato deliberately exaggerated to prove a point, or to make his story more mysterious or entertaining. This often happens, as stories get passed from generation to generation, much like a fish story in which the fish becomes larger and more ferocious with each telling. Scholars feel that Plato embellished the story of the civilization to make it seem older and far more grandiose than it actually was.

One of the first to notice the problem of Plato's time schedule was a man named Immanuel Velikovsky (1895–1979), who

Ruins of a temple in Sbeitla, Tunisia. Several Atlantean theorists placed the fabled land in this country.

proposed his theories in 1950. Velikovsky believed that Plato simply added "one too many zeroes" to his year count to exaggerate the age of the great nation. The island that Plato described, Velikovsky said, could very well have existed 900 years before Plato told the story, and to Velikovsky this made the best sense.

Not long after Velikovsky presented his ideas, a man named Jürgen Spanuth started researching Plato's claim that the story of Atlantis originated in Egypt with Egyptian priests who told the story to Solon, who in turn passed the story to others. After studying Egyptian temple inscriptions and papyrus texts, Spanuth stated that Egyptians felt each month was in itself a "year," and so, counting up the months that would span back far enough in time, we'd end up with 8,000 or 9,000 months ("years"). This would be the right time for the Egyptian priests to pass on the story, and for 900 years to pass before Plato could retell the story. Unfortunately, there's no real proof to support this idea.

Still others felt that Plato erred not on the side of exaggeration, but on that of underexaggeration. One such person was a Russian mystic named Madame Helena Petrovna Blavatsky (1831–1891). There's more about her and her theories in chapter five. But for now, it's enough to say that she believed, as did her followers, that Atlantis began to sink several million years ago and that it completed its final descent into the ocean about 850,000 years ago—stating that Plato should have *added* a couple of zeros, making his figure 900,000 years. It would, she said, have been more accurate!

Later, a German named Albert Herrmann (1886–1945) stated that Plato's numbers were off by a factor of 30, and he manipulated the number to show that if one divided 9,000 by 30, the date could feasibly locate Atlantis in the place that he felt it should be, Tunisia.

With all this number stretching you can't help getting confused about when the destruction of Atlantis occurred. To combat this problem, many researchers simply avoided this problem altogether, deciding to look instead at *where* Atlantis might have been, as opposed to *when.*

3

Could Atlantis Just Be a Dream?

Was Atlantis real, or was it a figment of Plato's imagination? There are many people who feel that Plato made up the whole story to prove a point. As a philosopher, Plato always came up with ideas of how society could be better and tried to convince his fellow citizens to follow those ideas. What, he wondered, would it take to create an ideal civilization—one based on a philosophy of wisdom and understanding?

To prove the theory that Plato made up the Atlantis story, scholars point out that Plato's description of Atlantis smacks of exaggeration. To quote him, he says in his work *Timaeus*:

Our records tell how your city checked a great power which arrogantly advanced from its base in the Atlantic Ocean to attack the cities of Europe and Asia. For in those days the Atlantic was navigable. There was an island opposite the strait which are by you (or so you say) called the Pillars of Hercules, an island larger than Libya and Asia combined.

The size of the island, which Plato states is larger than Libya and Asia combined, is almost too large to believe. How could such a large piece of land sink, never to be seen again? Most geologists find this idea absurd and deny that such an event could take place overnight or as quickly as Plato infers.

Historians also note that no other author of Plato's time speaks of Atlantis. Surely if it had been a real place, historians or writers of other cultures would have mentioned the destruction of such a great civilization in earlier writings than those of Plato. Yet not even the ancient and widely traveled Greek historian Herodotus (484–430 BC) mentions the story, and he, preceding Plato by only thirty years, is reputed to have spoken to those very Egyptian priests who supposedly passed along the story to Solon. However, Herodotus wrote that the Phoenicians were the first Greeks to undertake sea voyages, and that they were the first to pass the Strait of Gibraltar.

Aristotle refuted Plato's claims that Atlantis ever existed.

It is believed that Plato knew of Herodotus's writings about these voyages, and that he used that knowledge to help fashion his tale.

Plato's own student, Aristotle, states that Atlantis did not exist, but that the waters outside the Pillars of Hercules, where Atlantis was supposed to have sunk, are strangely shallow. Two hundred years later, Plutarch (AD 46–AD 120), another philosopher, said that Plato embellished the story originally passed to him to make it more of a fairy tale. According to Plutarch, it had been a much simpler and more believable story at the outset.

There are some, though, who feel that earlier stories do not exist because Plato gave the name Atlantis to a real place for which there was no known name, or at least a name that wasn't familiar to the Greeks. Could one of these ancient, nameless (to the Greeks) cultures be Atlantis? Some scientists think so, and many have offered theories of where and when such a culture may have existed. Another, less scientific theory presents the mythical island of Mu in Asia, which stories say was also destroyed in a fiery cataclysm. Still others claim more varied locations, like parts of the Sahara Desert, to be the ill-fated country.

In 1969, however, J. V. Luce (1920–), a historian, made an interesting case for an element of truth to Plato's tale. He made a very sound argument that Plato's description of Atlantis, while embellished, could have been based on a very real story—the story of the great volcanic destruction of the Greek island of Santorini, an island near Crete. We'll go into Santorini's story in more detail in chapter six; but apparently, it is noted in Egyptian literature that all trade with Crete was suddenly cut off, and the story of the disaster was relayed to Egypt by way of sailors and survivors. Like the party game "Telephone," in which a story is passed from person to person and usually changes with each retelling, Solon might have heard the story and passed it on to others, and eventually the tale could have come to Plato. Luce

Minoan artwork from ancient Crete, where some theories place Atlantis's origin. The Minoan Empire of the sixth century BC produced advanced art and science.

concludes that the Minoan Empire of Crete in the sixth century BC could very well be the basis for the story of Atlantis.

But even after Luce's theory was published, it didn't stop many scholarly—and some not-so-scholarly—people from letting their imaginations run wild with the story of an ideal world that had tragically found its end.

4

Many Theories and Theorists

People of all walks of life have tried to uncover the secrets of Atlantis. Atlantean scholars come in the form of oceanographers, archaeologists, geologists, mystics, poets, sociologists, and even politicians!

What is it about this story that draws people of such different backgrounds to it? What conclusions have they reached, and how close to the truth are they?

One of the first modern writers to look to Atlantis for inspiration was the English statesman, scientist, and philosopher Sir Francis Bacon (1561–1626). He wrote a fanciful tale entitled *The New Atlantis,* which placed the lost country in the New World of his time: America. In his story, some members of the Atlantean kingdom had survived the tragedy by building an ark and journeying across the waters to a new land they called Bensalem. Very few scholars consider Bacon's story to be little more than a flight of fancy.

Hollywood's *Siren of Atlantis* was based on a nineteenth-century French novel.

After Bacon's, more "scientific" theories started to fly from the pens of eager theorists. A Frenchman, Felix Berlioux (1828–1910), claimed in 1874 to have found the ruins of Atlantis at the foot of Morocco's Atlas Mountains near Casablanca. His theory inspired a novel called *L'Atlantide,* by Pierre Benoît, that tells the story of two Frenchmen who find a living Atlantis in the mountains of southern Algeria. The novel was so popular that it was translated into English and published in America under the title *The Queen of Atlantis*. Later, it was made into a movie no less than three times, as a silent film in

1921, as an early "talkie" in Germany in 1932, and in heyday Hollywood of 1948 as the film *Siren of Atlantis*.

In the early part of the twentieth century, Claude Roux, another Frenchman, placed Atlantis in the Mediterranean coast of Northwest Africa, which he said at one time was a fertile area. The location, he stated, was invaded so many times that the residents collectively forgot their history and their Atlantean origins.

Meanwhile, Count Byron Kuhn de Porok felt Atlantis was in the Sahara Desert and claimed to have found traces of it there, including a body of Tin Hinan—the main character of Pierre Benoît's novel. Needless to say, it wasn't the fictional Tin Hinan, but only the remains of a local dignitary.

Others felt that they had found Atlantis when in fact they had found something else entirely. One such man was Paul Borchardt, a geologist, who found the remains of a palace in Tunisia that he claimed was Atlantis. It was actually a Roman fortress—a valuable find, but certainly not what he'd anticipated. Albert Herrmann also found ancient irrigation works in Tunisia and wildly theorized that these had to have been part of an Atlantean colony that had come from the Netherlands! Unfortunately for Herrmann, it was not.

One of the most famous Atlantean scholars was not a scientist but a politician with a keen interest in the lost continent. Ignatius Donnelly (1831–1901) published his book, *Atlantis: The Antediluvian World* in 1882, after which the study of Atlantis became the talk of the nineteenth-century world. His theories about Atlantis were extremely imaginative and inspiring, and his book was so well received that for nearly a century he was considered the primary source on Atlantis, even though his theories had, to put it mildly, very little scientific truth.

Donnelly states that Plato did not invent Atlantis, and that his story is historically accurate. Atlantis was exactly where Plato had described it, in the mouth of the Mediterranean Sea. There, man grew to be civilized, colonizing regions around the globe including the Gulf of Mexico, the Mississippi River, the Amazon, the Pacific coast of South America, the Mediterranean, the west coasts of Europe and Africa, the Baltic Sea, the Black Sea, and the Caspian Sea.

Donnelly also believed that Atlantis was paradise. It was the Garden of Eden, the Elysian Fields (the ancient Grecian paradise), Mount Olympus (the home of the gods in Greek legend) and Asgard (the home of the gods in Norse legend), as well as many other focal points of religious belief. There, mankind had been peaceful and happy for generations. Additionally, the gods and goddesses of most ancient cultures were the kings, queens, and heroes of Atlantis.

Egypt, Donnelly says, was formed as an Atlantean colony, and Atlantean iron and bronze tools were the first to appear on Earth. Our alphabet, which comes to us from the Phoenicians, was inspired by Atlanteans, as were those of the Maya in Central America. Their race spawned most of the races on Earth. When Atlantis sunk cataclysmically into the ocean, some escaped on ships and rafts and went to other nations telling of the disaster, spawning the many legends of the Great Flood.

This sixteenth-century artwork depicts the gods and goddesses on Mount Olympus, believed by some Atlantean scholars to have been Atlantis.

Even today, the story of Atlantis captures people's imaginations. The Disney film *Atlantis: The Lost Empire* opened children's minds to the story in 2001.

One can see just by reading Donnelly's theories why they were so popular. They explain practically every mystery of the ancient world in one fell swoop. In later years, scientists would disprove most of his statements. Geologists have proven, for instance, that Atlantis did not sink into the ocean the way that Donnelly said. Landmasses, while they can sink, take thousands and millions of years to do so. Even the fastest-sinking landmasses could not possibly do it as quickly as Plato and Donnelly claim Atlantis did. The only way it could happen, even theoretically, is in a small area no bigger than a few miles, as a result of an earthquake or a volcanic eruption. Nothing on the scale of what Plato described would be possible.

Even so, Donnelly's theories still have a following today and have been the basis for many films, novels, television shows, comic books, and other works of art.

One of Donnelly's fans, Lewis Spence (1874–1955), was probably one of the most prolific and well-known of the Atlantis scholars. Spence, a news reporter, expounded on his predecessor's theories, stating that an entire continent once spanned America and Europe, and that when it sank, it left several islands in its wake— namely the Canaries, the Azores, Madiera, and the West Indies. He also stated that the people of Atlantis, who spawned all the races of the world, were exceptionally tall—a type of master race. Spence, however, hated Nazi Germany, which had risen to power in his time, and stated emphatically that Nazi Germany would fall for the same reason that Atlantis fell—corruption.

Other Atlantean theorists actually paved the way for genuine scientific research with their theories. Although they didn't lead us anywhere closer to Atlantis, they brought to light things about our world that we did not know previously.

One example of this was from Professor Pierre Termier of Paris who believed, as many did, that Atlantis had sunk and that its lands lay beneath the Atlantic Ocean. In 1915, he set about describing these lands beneath the ocean from what he knew of the ocean at the time, and came surprisingly close to describing exactly what we now refer to as the Mid-Atlantic Ridge of mountains, which were not found until the 1940s. Modern oceanographers know that the Mid-Atlantic Ridge was, and always has been, a mountain range formed by volcanic action and not a sunken continent. Termier had miraculously figured out it was there, without ever seeing it.

Another scientific discovery that came to light from the theories of Atlantis is "continental drift," or the fact that the continents move and shift location very slowly. Alfred Wegener introduced this theory in 1915 and was summarily laughed at by his peers. Years later, Atlantologists latched onto his ideas, and when other scientists took a hard look at his findings, they realized Wegener was right. The Atlantologists proved nothing about Atlantis, but they brought notoriety to a scientific theory that sorely needed it.

Atlantologists still love this theory. In 1995 Rand and Rose Flem-Ath used the premise in their attempt to prove that Atlantis

One theory places Atlantis beneath the Antarctic ice sheet.

was actually the frozen continent of Antarctica. They theorized that due to continental drift, a sheet of ice drifted over the continent, and that it rests there today, buried beneath the ice. Considered highly unlikely by most geologists, their hypothesis has not been researched in detail.

Meanwhile, other theorists have tried to explain the myth of Atlantis. Charles Berlitz (1913–), the grandson of the founder of the Berlitz travel guides company, wrote a book on the Bermuda Triangle, in which he proposed that some of the strange happenings in that area might be by-products of the type of event that caused Atlantis to sink beneath the ocean.

Others, like Immanuel Velikovsky (mentioned in chapter two) suggested that Atlantis was destroyed by something greater than a flood or a volcano. Velikovsky was of the opinion that an extraterrestrial event caused destruction on Earth. He believed that Venus, acting as a comet, swung too close to Earth and caused the catastrophic disruption on Earth's surface. His ideas were (and still are) considered a bit far-fetched to say the least, but he points to ancient sources that describe similar incidents of ancient volcanic activity, in Mayan and Egyptian texts as well as those of the Bible. He also quotes *Timaeus*, in which Plato writes of periods in which the paths of the planets varied and caused widespread destruction on Earth.

If true, such a cataclysmic event would have left an indelible mark on the minds of those who survived it. How is it, we wonder, that someone from that time did not find a way of communicating the story in more detail? Velikovsky explains this away as a form of mass amnesia. The incidents, he says, were too horrible to remember so the human race simply forgot about it.

How can anyone prove or disprove that?

5

The Mystical
and the Magical

Today, there are many stories about Atlantis and its people—people who are no longer exactly human. We read comic books like *Aquaman* and *Sub-Mariner,* and see a people who can breathe under water and speak with undersea life. In other stories, television shows, and movies we see people who control great magic, or who are different than we are in many alien ways—they have mental powers, strange physical characteristics, and enormous physical strength.

Do these ideas about a race with unusual traits have any basis in fact? Some say yes. Ignatius Donnelly started the tradition by writing that Atlantis was the true paradise described by many religions of the world, and that many cultures and languages of Earth found their origins in Atlantis.

One of the earliest Atlantis spiritualists was Madame Helena Petrovna Blavatsky, who was mentioned in chapter two. After coming to New York City in 1871, Madame Blavatsky gained a great following in the last twenty years of the nineteenth century, claiming that her spiritual advisor, Koot Hoomie, a Hindu master, sent her letters telling her about an ancient history of the world. (It was later discovered that she was writing them to herself.) Madame Blavatsky promoted the belief that there were many ancient "root" races on Earth, only one of which was the Atlanteans. Atlanteans, she claimed, were the fourth race of man, who were preceded by the third race: the Lemurians—who were fifteen feet tall, with eyes so far apart that they could see sideways, and whose heels were so long they could walk backwards as well as forwards. Humans, Blavatsky believed, are the fifth race of man on Earth.

Some of the most interesting mystical looks at Atlantis come by way of psychics. There have been many mystics over the years who have claimed a psychic connection to Atlantis. One such psychic, named Dion Fortune (1890–1946) claimed she saw Atlantis in a vision when she was only four years old. After she died, another psychic, named Gareth Knight (1930–), stated that he learned about Atlantis from Dion Fortune, who'd visited him as a spirit. Knight confirmed that the Atlanteans were a different race from humans, and that they were seven feet tall and had a softer, sponge-like quality to their skin. Another psychic, named Christine Hartley, who worked extensively on the belief in reincarnation, believed that Atlanteans grew so much in intelligence and mental powers that they outgrew their moral development.

Most of these psychics claimed to be channeling spirits from Atlantis, or receiving their information from the world beyond. One of the most famous psychics of the twentieth century, Edgar Cayce (pronounced "Casey") was no exception. Cayce put himself into hypnotic trances, and in this state, he'd communicate all that he was learning from the spirit world. Born in 1877, Cayce learned of this ability as a youth when he had a throat illness that caused him to lose his voice. A friend offered to cure him by putting him in a hypnotic trance, and under hypnosis Cayce was able to speak normally. As he grew older, he treated people by putting them in hypnotic trances and prescribing treatments. He claimed to be able read a person's aura, or halo of energy around his or her body, and diagnose ailments from it. He became known around the country for his miraculous cures.

A beach on the east side of North Bimini. According to late psychic Edgar Cayce, Bimini
is the peak of one of Atlantis's mountain ranges.

In his trances, Cayce stated he could see into the past and predict the future. He predicted the destruction of Los Angeles, San Francisco and New York, the conversion of China to democracy, the destruction of Japan (sliding into the sea), and the end of Communism in Russia. All of this was to happen before 1998. Only the last prediction has come to pass, but many believed Cayce— especially when it came to Atlantis.

Cayce studied 1,600 people, and from the psychic "life readings" of those people, he predicted the reemergence of Atlantis. Apparently half of the people were, in his opinion, reincarnated citizens of the fabled lost continent. He believed that the souls of Atlantis were returning to Earth to bring about great change. He would hear the words of these reincarnated souls in a trancelike state and have them transcribed. From these transcriptions, he revealed what happened to Atlantis, according to those who lived there.

According to these ancient spirits, the world at the time of Atlantis was topsy-turvy—the northern portion of Earth was the southern portion. The Nile opened into the Atlantic Ocean, and the Sahara was a fertile land. That the Sahara was once fertile is fact; we have no geologic evidence to back up the rest of the "spirits'" claims.

Cayce passed away in 1945, but before he died he revealed what the spirits told him was the exact location of the fabled lost continent. Atlantis, Cayce stated, was a massive continent sitting between the Gulf of Mexico and the Mediterranean Sea. The British West Indies, or the Bahamas, or Bimini, are some of what remain of its vast mountain ranges. Cayce also stated that a great cataclysm destroyed Atlantis. Its civilization was so technologically advanced that it harnessed atomic energy and invented flying machines 50,000 years ago. Survivors of the destruction spread across the world and gave their achievements to ancient civilizations like the Egyptians. He said they buried their most important documents under the paws of the Sphinx in Egypt.

Based on what he said the souls of Atlantis told him, Cayce predicted that Atlantis would rise again around the year 1968. Hearing this prophesy, several people mounted expeditions to the Bahamas to look in the areas Cayce had indicated, waiting for the rising fabled land. Two of his followers were Robert Ferro and Michael Grumley, who located an underwater grouping of geometrically shaped rocks near the coast of Bimini that they felt was proof of an underwater city. Sadly, these two gentlemen claimed their inspiration through the questionable influences of tarot cards and marijuana, so their findings were suspect.

Following up on their apparent discovery, Dr. David Zink, another one of Cayce's enthusiasts and an expert scuba diver, organized three expeditions in 1975, 1976, and 1977 in which he dived over and photographed the stones in question. He claimed they had the appearance of buildings, and that one could almost see streets in the way they were laying along the seabed. He declared they were columns, and that they showed the definite remains of a lost civilization.

Oceanographers discovered this deep sea garden of hot springs and towering spires 3,000 feet below the Atlantic Ocean. They nicknamed it the Lost City.

After studying the stones, however, oceanographers and geologists explained that it is not unusual for undersea stone formations near beach rock to break in straight lines and right angles, giving the appearance of buildings. These rocks, as it turns out, are shaped naturally based on the environment, and not the fabled Atlantis rising from the sea.

In 1967, shortly before Cayce's followers were turning the Bahamas upside down searching for proof of Atlantis's resurrection, Greek archaeologist Spyridon Marinatos (1901–1974) began excavating on a volcanic island in the Mediterranean. There he uncovered the capital of an ancient civilization that made all Atlantean scholars and researchers take notice. Had Atlantis truly risen again—on the island of Santorini?

6

Where Is the Legend Today?

After all the wild theories, most of which are based on decidedly shaky science, modern science may have found a clue in the search for Atlantis. Recently, study of the legend has centered on the Greek islands of Crete and Santorini in the Sea of Crete (where the Aegean Sea and the Mediterranean Sea meet). Santorini, also called Santorin and Thera, is the southernmost island of the Cyclades group of islands. It is a semicircular island, all that remains of an exploded volcano—a volcano that reputedly erupted around the year 1620 BC. Separated by only sixty miles, the islands of Crete and Thera/Santorini housed a mysterious ancient people that we now refer to as the Minoans.

About 2,500 years ago, this extremely powerful and successful culture ruled the region. Threatened only by their aggressive Greek neighbors, the Mycenaeans, they remained solidly rooted for a thousand years.

A town in Thera/Santorini, an island that is the remnant of an ancient volcano

What's really strange about these people is how they suddenly appeared as if from nowhere, and then suddenly disappeared. Archaeologists in the latter half of the twentieth century have been uncovering more clues about them and their sudden disappearance, and finding possible links between them and Plato's tale of Atlantis.

Eight thousand years ago, the first settlers of Crete arrived on the island's shores. Archaeologists have uncovered the settlers' remains, and have found that they were a small and slender people, very similar to the people of the Mediterranean today. Archaeologists also found remains of a different people, however, a taller and shorterskulled race, which apparently joined the previous population of Crete around 2500 BC with little or no violence.

In 1866, on the island of Santorini, a French volcanologist, Ferdinand Foqué, was studying the volcano that had erupted there, and he heard about two mysterious tombs hidden in the hardened lava. Enlisting the aid of some archaeologists, he uncovered the first Minoan remains to come to light for 2,500 years. He found a crypt with a central pillar made of blocks of lava, human skeletons, blades made of obsidian, and pottery that was decorated in a style that no one had seen before. After some study, he found that a volcanic eruption around 2000 BC had blown the island apart—separating it into three islands that remain in the Santorini group of islands today. His research showed that a volcanic eruption of this magnitude would have been heard as far away as Gibraltar, Scandinavia, the Arabian Sea, and Central Africa. It would have created tidal waves of mythic proportion, sending them crashing down on the nearby islands, including the island of Crete, and would have rocked them with earthquakes, darkening the sky and smothering them with volcanic ash.

An example of how large a tidal wave a volcano can create was witnessed in 1883, with the eruption of the volcano Krakatau, or Krakatoa, which sent 135-foot waves to the nearby coasts of Java and Sumatra, flooding more than 300 towns and villages and drowning nearly 36,000 people.

Realizing that Foqué's team had discovered a civilization older than that of the Mycenaeans, a British archaeologist named Arthur Evans (1851–1941) went to Crete to see if he could find more evidence of this culture on that island. On Crete, Evans uncovered a huge palace, which he believed to be the home of King Minos, the legendary ruler of Crete in Greek mythology. In honor of King Minos, he named the ancient race of people who had built that palace and the surrounding area settlement "Minoans." Study of the palace showed that it had been severely damaged by earthquakes and other natural disasters. After these disasters had greatly weakened the Minoans, scientists believe the Mycenaeans invaded Minoan territory, claiming it for their own.

In 1967 Spyridon Marinatos, the Greek archaeologist mentioned in chapter five, decided to dig in a part of Santorini known as Akrotiri. In 1939, he had theorized that the eruption of Thera, the ash and pumice of which have been found as far away as Egypt and Israel, was the inspiration for the legend of Atlantis.

Tourists walk through the ancient site of Akrotiri on the Cyclades island of Santorini.

He chose Akrotiri to further explore this theory, and there he uncovered an extensive Minoan city that could only have been a thriving, powerful one. At Akrotiri, multileveled buildings were discovered, as well as a high level of culture and art that was greater in size than what had been found by the earlier archaeological work on Crete and Santorini. Akrotiri, Marinatos believed, was the real capital of the Minoan civilization, because of the incredible palaces that were uncovered and the expanse of the settlement. What was most amazing about the find was that it confirmed that this location was completely leveled by a volcano, and it focused the time period of the event to the year at or around 1500 BC, exactly 1000 years after the Minoans appeared on Crete.

The language of the Minoans, it was discovered, was an early form of Greek. Although two scholars named John Chadwick (1920–) and Michael Ventris (1922–1956) managed to decipher some of it, we have none of the Minoans' stories, histories, or literature. We do not even have their name for themselves, for all the items available for translation were simple lists and ledgers. Nothing else was written down, at least not on materials that lasted. For this reason, the Minoans remain a nameless, mysterious, brilliant people—a people who were once a world power.

Could this elusive people, this great nation, be the origin for Plato's story? Only further scientific study will tell the tale. The time period does not match Plato's story, but surely a great civilization such as the one found on Crete and Santorini could have posed a threat to the ancient Greeks as Plato proposed—and its cataclysmic death could have inspired his story. We may never know the truth. Atlantis hides its secrets very well. There is no doubt the mystery and glamour of the story will inspire many others to search for the tragic, fabled land. Someday, one of them just may find it.

Glossary

Aegean Sea A sea that joins the Mediterranean Sea, through the Sea of Crete. It touches the shores of Greece.

Akrotiri An ancient settlement on the island of Santorini, in the Sea of Crete.

anthropologist A scientist who studies human beings; in particular, their origin, classification, relationship of races, physical characteristics, environmental and social relations, and culture.

archaeologist A scientist who studies material remains (as fossil relics, artifacts, and monuments) of past human life and activities.

Atlantean One who would reside in Atlantis.

Atlantean scholar One who studies the legend of Atlantis and publishes his or her findings.

Atlantic The ocean that touches the eastern shores of the Americas, and the western shores of Europe and Africa.

Atlantis A legendary continent or island described by the ancient philosopher Plato, which was destroyed by a terrible natural disaster, sinking into the ocean.

cataclysm A natural disaster of grand proportion.

continental drift The scientific theory that continents actually move or drift.

Crete A Greek island in the Aegean Sea.

Critias The name of one of Plato's associates, who told the story of Atlantis to Plato. It is also the title of one of Plato's dialogues.

geologist One who studies minerals, their formation, and their movement and changes in the earth.

idyllic Perfect; something that is completely without flaw.

Mid-Atlantic Ridge A ridge of mountains that lies beneath the Atlantic Ocean.

Minoans An ancient race of people that mysteriously disappeared in the year 1500 BC. Most recent study has led scientists to believe that they might have been the origin for the Atlantis legend.

Mycenaeans An ancient people related to the Greeks who were the competitors of the Minoans.

philosopher Someone who seeks wisdom or enlightenment.

Pillars of Hercules Rock formations flanking the Strait of Gibraltar.

Plato An ancient Greek philosopher, who introduced the legend of Atlantis.

psychic Someone who explores topics outside the realm of physical science, such as paranormal incidents and spirits.

reincarnation The belief that the spirit of one who dies is reborn in another person or creature.

Santorini Another name for Thera, an island neighboring Crete in the Sea of Crete. It is the southern half of an exploded volcano.

Sea of Crete A sea that joins the Aegean Sea to the Mediterranean Sea.

sociologist A scientist who studies the development, structure, interaction, and collective behavior of organized groups of human beings.

Socrates A philosopher, and Plato's teacher.

spiritualist One who believes spirits of the dead communicate with the living, usually through a medium.

Thera Another name for the island of Santorini in the Sea of Crete. It is the southern half of an exploded volcano.

Timaeus One of Plato's dialogues, which explores the legend of Atlantis.

volcanologist A scientist who studies volcanoes.

For More Information

American Museum of Natural History
Central Park West at 79th Street
New York, NY 10024-5192
(212) 769-5000
Web sites: http://nimidi.amnh.org/
　　　　　 http://www.amnh.org/

Archaeological Institute of America
Located at Boston University
656 Beacon Street, Fourth Floor
Boston, MA 02215-2006
(617) 353-9361
Web site: http://www.archaeological.org/

The Franck Goddio Society (undersea exploration)
1100 Oneok Plaza
100 West Fifth Street
Tulsa, OK 74103-4217
Web sites: http://www.franckgoddio.org
　　　　　 http://www.underwaterdiscovery.org/

Institute of Human Origins (anthropology and archaeology)
Arizona State University
P.O. Box 874101
Tempe, AZ 85287-4101
(480) 727-6580
Web site: http://www.asu.edu/clas/iho/

CANADA

Canadian Archaeological Association
Department of Anthropology and Archaeology
University of Saskatchewan
55 Campus Drive
Saskatoon, SK S7N 5B1
(306) 966-4188
Web site: http://www.canadianarchaeology.com/

WEB SITES

Atlantis Discovered
http://www.atlantisdiscovered.org/

Atlantis: Fact, Fiction or Exaggeration
http://www.atlantisrising.com/index.html

Disney's *Atlantis: The Lost Empire*
http://disney.go.com/disneypictures/atlantis/flash/index.html

Excite on Atlantis—Santorini and the Legend of Atlantis
http://www.geo.aau.dk/palstrat/tom/santorini_homepage/atlantis.htm

For Further Reading

Balit, Christina. *Atlantis: The Legend of a Lost City.* New York: Henry Holt, 2000.

Bowman, John S. *The Quest for Atlantis.* Garden City, NY: Doubleday, 1971.

Braymer, Marjorie. *Atlantis, the Biography of a Legend.* New York: Atheneum, 1983.

Crawford, Sue. *Lands of Legend.* New York: Bookwright Press, 1989.

DeCamp, L. Sprague. *Lost Continents: The Atlantis Theme in History, Science, and Literature.* New York: Dover, 1970.

Ellis, Richard. *Imagining Atlantis.* New York: Alfred A. Knopf, 1998.

Luce, John Victer. *Lost Atlantis: New Light on an Old Legend.* New York: McGraw-Hill 1969.

Pellegrino, Charles. *Unearthing Atlantis.* New York: Random House, 1991.

Plato. *The Collected Dialogues of Plato.* New York: Pantheon, 1961.

Index

ABOUT THE AUTHOR

Ann Margaret Lewis attended Michigan State University and began her career writing children's stories, comic stories, and activity books for DC Comics. She has contributed to several media magazines, books, and Web sites, and presently works as a Web producer. Ms. Lewis lives in the Bronx, New York, with her husband, Joseph, and her very talkative orange tabby cat named Camille.

PHOTO CREDITS

Cover © David Hardy/Photo Researchers; p. 4 © PhotoDisc; p. 6 © Hulton Archive; p. 7 © FPG International; p. 9 © Mimmo Jodice/Corbis; p. 11 © Hans Georg Roth/Corbis; p. 16 © Corbis; p. 18 © Buddy Mays/Corbis; pp. 20, 24 © The Everett Collection; p. 23 © Arte & Immagini srl/Corbis; p. 27 © Wolfgang Kaehler/Corbis; p. 32 © Tony Arruza/Corbis; p. 35 © AP/Wide World Photos; pp. 37, 40 © Gail Mooney/Corbis.

SERIES DESIGN AND LAYOUT

Geri Giordano